ALL ABOUT **THE JUNGLE**

ALL
ABOUT

THE
JUNGLE

Written and Illustrated by

Armstrong Sperry

allabout
books

**RANDOM
HOUSE**
NEW YORK

FIRST PRINTING

© COPYRIGHT, 1959, BY ARMSTRONG SPERRY

LIBRARY OF CONGRESS CATALOG CARD NUMBER: 59-6458

MANUFACTURED IN THE UNITED STATES OF AMERICA

CONTENTS

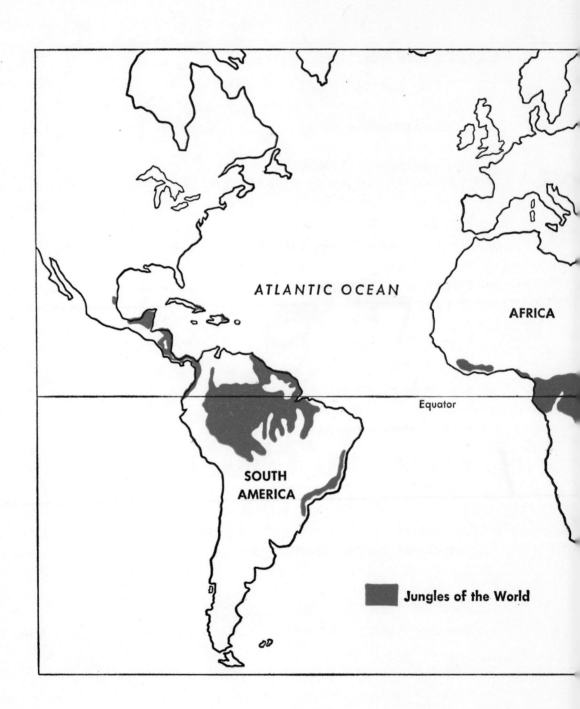

ATLANTIC OCEAN

AFRICA

Equator

SOUTH
AMERICA

Jungles of the World

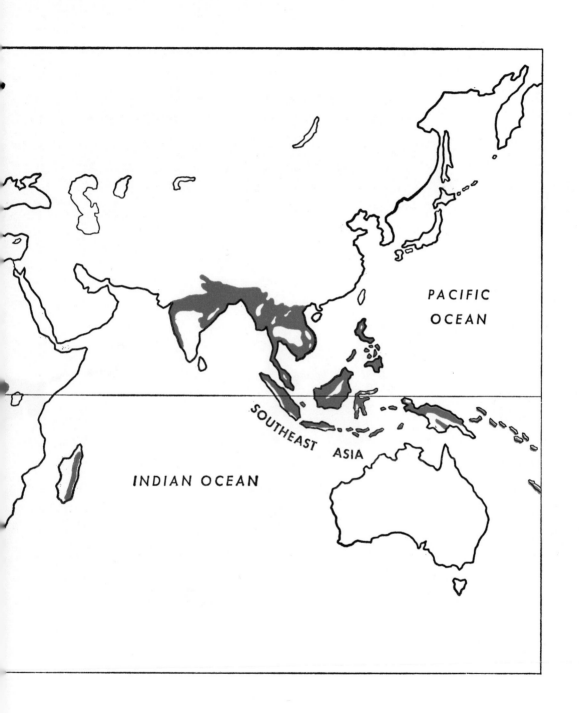

PACIFIC
OCEAN

INDIAN OCEAN

SOUTHEAST ASIA

AUTHOR'S NOTE

I would like to thank the following for their helpful suggestions about this book: W. Wedgwood Bowen, professor of zoology, Dartmouth College; Frank C. Craighead, Jr., wildlife biologist, U.S. Fish and Wildlife Service, co-author of *How to Survive on Land and Sea* (United States Naval Institute); and Kenneth P. Emory, ethnologist, the Bernice P. Bishop Museum of Honolulu, author of *South Sea Lore*.

ARMSTRONG SPERRY
Hanover, New Hampshire

ALL ABOUT **THE JUNGLE**

1

JUNGLES AROUND THE WORLD

Once upon a time, our whole planet was covered with dense, tangled masses of vegetation called jungle. With the approach of the first ice ages, millions of years ago, the vast forests began to retreat. The hardier trees —evergreens, maples, and oaks—somehow held their own against the enemy ice.

But today true jungle may be found only in the belt of lands encircling the equator. There it covers one-tenth of the world's total land surface, and nearly one-half of the total forest areas of the earth.

The largest of these jungle regions is found in South America. There it fills more than a million square miles of the Amazon and Guiana river valleys. It extends from the Mato Grosso of Brazil to the Caribbean shore. It is found also in Central America and southern Mexico.

In the Far East, jungle country extends from southwestern India to Indochina and the Philippines. The largest area of continuous jungle in this far part of the world lies in the Malay Peninsula and the adjoining islands of Indonesia.

The enormous jungle region of West Africa is second in size to that of Brazil. From the Congo basin it extends westward into French Equatorial Africa.

In these widely scattered jungle areas, there are far more differences in plant and animal life than in the human races that dwell in them. But one factor unites them all—a similar climate. The burning sun creates masses of heated air. This air rises, cools, and gives off its water content as rain. Avalanches of water strike down at the jungle—an annual average that may reach as much as a hundred inches. Cloudbursts may account for thirty inches of water in as many days. This is why botanists call jungle country the Rain Forest.

In regions close to the equator, there are two rainy seasons a year. These alternate with two so-called dry

The jungle has a hot, steamy climate.

seasons. During the dry seasons, four or five inches of rain may fall during a single month. Even under fair skies the treetops of the Rain Forest give off an endless drip, drip, drip.

In the jungle the air is always dank and steamy. This is because the dense foliage cuts off sun and wind. The moisture has no chance to evaporate. Under such hothouse conditions, trees and plants grow luxuriantly.

The average annual temperature of the Rain Forest is 80° Fahrenheit. But the heat of noonday may soar many degrees above that. Night temperatures may drop as low as 62°, but this is exceptional.

Contrary to popular belief, the tropics do not hold the record for high temperatures. These are found in desert areas such as the California desert, where the heat may be as great as 130° in the shade.

Some people think that the great tropical jungles are almost impossible for a person to make his way through. There are even stories of men using machetes to hack their way. This is true in many places. But where the first growth of trees has remained undisturbed, there is no tangle of new trees, vines, and shrubs. The trunks of the highest trees have branches only at the top. The ground between the trees is quite open. It is carpeted with a thin layer of leaves that fall unceasingly the year around. This is especially true of regions that are well drained, and where the unbroken mass of treetops lets little sunlight filter down.

The thick, matted jungle, seen so often in the movies or on television, is what botanists call "secondary growth." This is jungle that has sprung up in places which have once been cleared by man. It is very often dense and brushy.

In the Rain Forest, jungle trees grow to three different levels. The treetops form three great layers, one above the other, in somewhat the same way that cloud masses build higher and higher upon other clouds.

The tallest trees may grow to be as much as two hundred feet tall. They are known as "emergents" because they have been the first to break through and reach the sunlight.

Beneath them grows a level of shorter trees, sixty to 125 feet high. These form the dense, interweaving canopy of the Rain Forest ceiling.

Secondary growth is a thick tangle of plants.

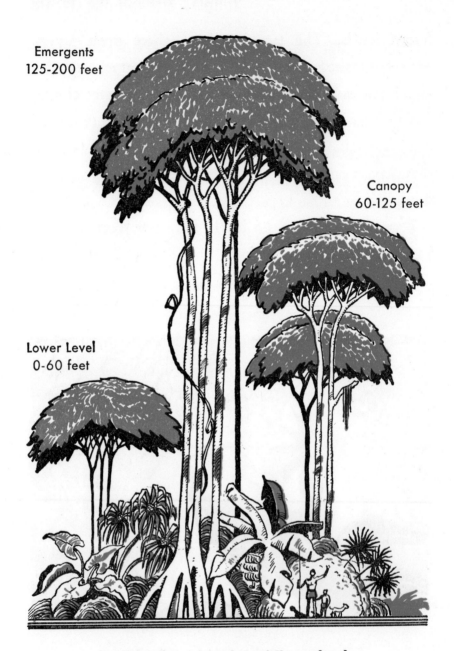

Emergents
125-200 feet

Canopy
60-125 feet

Lower Level
0-60 feet

Jungle trees grow to three different levels.

Beneath this second level lies a third—an undergrowth of shrubs and saplings and of moss-bearded tree ferns, which sometimes reach a height of sixty feet.

Each layer of the Rain Forest has its own special forms of plant and animal life.

At first glance, many of these trees show striking similarities in bark texture, leaf shape, and color. This is explained by the jungle's great age. For millions of years, the various tree and plant families have shared the same environment. They have been forced to make similar adjustments. Thus, over vast periods of time, they have developed along similar lines.

Everywhere in the jungle there are plants growing on, over, and around other plants. Probably the most common are the ropelike vines, called lianas. They twist like giant snakes. Sometimes they develop woody stems two feet thick and six hundred feet long. Overhead, they interlace from branch to branch, from treetop to treetop. Often the liana network is so dense that it holds a tree upright even after it has been chopped at the base.

Even more astonishing than the lianas are the air plants—orchids and lichens. These flourish high in the treetops away from the soil of earth. Their roots fasten upon cracks and crannies in the branches of trees. Soon they collect the dust of rotted vegetation, which slowly forms a nourishing soil of its own.

The dense foliage of the jungle becomes like a great spider web. Air roots from high branches grow down to find a foothold in the jungle floor. Some creepers are armed with spikes. Most give shelter to a horde of ants and spiders, scorpions and centipedes.

All jungle growth seems oversized. Relatives of periwinkles grow forty feet tall. Members of the violet's family grow to the size of pear trees. Verbena spreads branches like an oak. Bamboo (actually a grass) grows fifty to seventy feet high. It may shoot up as much as a foot in a single day.

In northern countries, the forest may show at most a few dozen varieties of trees. But a single square mile of the Rain Forest will disclose as many as two or three hundred different species.

In spite of the jungle's lush vegetation, however, the underlying soil is poor. This is because falling leaves decay very quickly. The dense network of roots absorbs the leaf food almost as quickly as it dissolves into the earth. When cleared of trees, most jungle soil is so poor that it can support crops for only one season.

Certain jungle trees produce blossoms on the trunk

or branches. These low-growing flowers are visited by billions of insects which could never climb to blossoms far above the forest floor. Each insect carries life-giving pollen from flower to flower. In other parts of the world, wind will carry pollen to the blossoms; but in the jungle, wind is almost unknown.

Termites, sometimes called white ants, play an important part in the life cycle of the jungle. They chew the wood of branches and limbs, of tree trunks that fall to the ground. Bacteria transform this "sawdust" into humus, and humus into nitrogen and mineral matter. Over the years, all living things—the highest trees, the toughest lianas, the most delicate leaves—drop to the earth to die. Finally they are dissolved in the drip, drip, drip of the endless rains.

THE BRAZILIAN

JUNGLE

2

TREES, VINES, AND RUBBER

From the air, the great Brazilian jungle looks like an endless green sea. Here and there it is cut by one river after another flowing into the Amazon. These are the only paths into the interior. The names of some of those jungle rivers tell their own story: River of Blood, River of Death, River of Doubt. But many of the rivers have no names. They are still uncharted and unexplored.

In all that tremendous region, few traces of man can be seen. There are few breaks in the massive green carpet of the forest. No single tree seems to reach upward above its fellows. No mountain peaks cast valley shade. There are no landmarks.

The Brazilian Jungle

In the Brazilian jungle there are more than 8000 species of trees. This is ten times the number in the whole United States.

Brazilian hardwoods are among the hardest in the world. Crowded together, they shoot straight up without a branch for fifteen times a man's height. But it is extremely difficult to move such wood. Most of these woods are so heavy that they will not float down a river. Because of their great weight, they sink like stones. Yet they cannot be moved by road because there are no roads, and the cost of building roads into the jungle is almost prohibitive.

Moreover, ordinary wood-cutting tools are useless against such iron-like timber. A circular saw may lose its teeth within a few seconds. An ax leaves scarcely a scratch on the bark. Such trees must be drilled as though they were made of steel. A fallen tree trunk, covered with generations of moss and leaf mold, may be as sound as on the day it fell.

One of the jungle trees is the calabash. Its fruit looks like green cannon balls dangling from the branches. The shells of this fruit are used as bowls, cups, and basins.

Another is the jacare. Its bark looks like crocodile

Rivers are the roadways into the Brazilian jungle.

hide. It is so hard that it cannot be eaten by termites, and is only very slowly destroyed by rot.

The buriti palm provides a fiber from which the Indians make their hammocks and arrow lashings.

The jatoba tree has bark three-quarters of an inch thick, which can be removed in one piece and shaped into a canoe.

The featherweight balsa is the lightest commercial wood known today. Its weight is half that of cork. It is used in making light plywood parts in airplane construction. River Indians use balsa to construct their rafts. Mature trees grow from sixty to ninety feet tall, with gray-and-white bark.

There are monumental "pigeon blood" mahogany trees, ebony, and cedars. One towering tree produces Brazil nuts.

The beautiful babassu palm has nuts that are shipped in great quantities to the United States and Europe. They are made into margarine, soap, oils, and medical products. Their shells are used in making dyes and other chemical products.

From the cashew tree, we get delicious nuts. Its fruit makes a tasty beverage. Oil from the cashew is used in airplane parts, as well as in brake linings.

Some trees yield valuable beans and berries: vegetable ivory for making buttons, castor beans and vanilla, cocoa and coffee. One kind of palm tree furnishes food, clothing, and shelter for the Indians and even the blowguns from which they shoot their poisoned darts.

For centuries, Indian witch doctors have used jungle plants that have healing powers. Some plants are deadly poison, but even these have been turned to good use.

For centuries, witch doctors have used quinine to fight malaria. It comes from the bark of the cinchona tree.

Jungle Indians have long used digitalis, derived from the foxglove plant, for heart ailments. Snakeroot, belladonna, and ipecac were all Indian cure-alls.

Sassafras was a sixteenth-century wonder drug that the first Spanish invaders carried back to Europe. From the bark of the Brazilian willow comes salicylate, used in making aspirin. To deaden aches and pains, Indians have always chewed the leaves of the coca plant. Today we use this plant to make cocaine. And dentists use a form of cocaine to ease the pain of pulling a tooth.

The poison known as curare has long been used by the Brazilian Indians to tip their darts and arrows for killing game. They also learned to use it in small quanti-

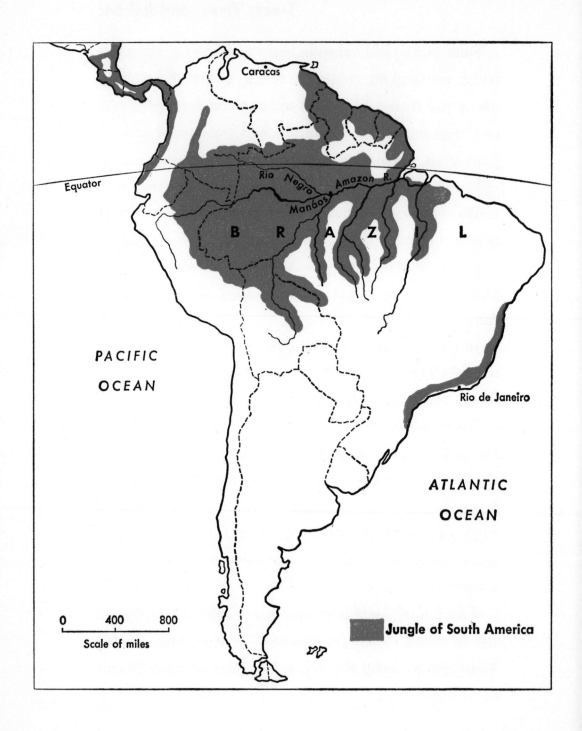

Caracas

Equator

Rio Negro Amazon R.

Manáos

B R A Z I L

PACIFIC

OCEAN

Rio de Janeiro

ATLANTIC

OCEAN

| 0 | 400 | 800 |

Scale of miles

Jungle of South America

ties to relieve muscular spasms. In 1938, a Canadian physician brought curare into North America for the first time. Today it is used throughout the world as a treatment for spastic paralysis. Our surgeons have found (just as the Indians did so long ago) that it is useful to relax tense muscles during operations.

Much of the antivenin for snakebite is prepared in Brazil. Scientists learned from the Indians that poison could be used to combat poison. For years the jungle men had been scratching their bodies cautiously with the fangs of poisonous snakes. In this way they made themselves immune to snakebite.

They have also used the sap of a vine known as timbo. This is a drug which, when thrown into the water, paralyzes fish and makes them easy to catch. From timbo modern scientists have evolved rotenone. It is used for killing insects but is harmless to human beings.

The early Spaniards found jungle Indians using a vegetable mold that was similar in its magic to our penicillin.

Today many of the leading drug companies of America are encouraging exploration in the Rain Forest. They are searching for medicinal plants which may still be unknown to us.

The Brazilian Jungle

The outside world owes a great debt to the Indians of the jungle, and to the invaluable products which grow there in such abundance.

One jungle plant deserves to be singled out above all others: the rubber tree. Its contribution to the development of modern civilization is tremendous. But the story of rubber has been a stormy one.

In the Brazilian jungle, the rubber tree is called hevea. It is a large tree, frequently a hundred feet tall. The hevea grows deep in the jungle. Taller trees protect it from the fierce heat of the sun. One hevea tree produces from five to fourteen pounds of rubber in a year.

For centuries the Indians have known how to tap the trees and catch the elastic sap known as latex.

Once it became known in Europe, dozens of uses were found for rubber. An enthusiastic Englishman discovered that a small ball of rubber would rub out pencil marks. Hence the name "rubber" became popular. The first hard-rubber bicycle tires were forerunners of tires for automobiles.

The years between 1900 and 1912 are a dark blot on the history of the jungle country of Brazil. As a result of the discovery and monopoly of rubber, millionaires sprang up overnight. Money was growing on trees—

Indians have long known how to tap rubber trees.

wild rubber trees that oozed a sticky substance as valuable as gold. On the edge of jungle rivers, mansions were built of marble imported from Italy. They were furnished in fine style.

In the booming town called Manáos, on the banks of the Rio Negro, a large opera house was erected. It was built in pieces in England at a cost of $10,000,000 and was carried across the Atlantic Ocean. The greatest singers of the day sang on its stage; for by that time Manáos had become one of the wealthiest cities in the

world. And why not? A single canoe-load of raw rubber—produced by the slave labor of jungle Indians—
was worth $2500.

Bringing rubber out of the jungle required the hardest kind of physical toil. But the rubber merchants did
none of this labor themselves. They captured Indians
by the thousands and made them slaves. The nearby
tribes found that their arrows were no match for bullets.
Indians who refused to follow orders were shot down,
beheaded, or flogged. There was no law to halt such
cruelty. News of these conditions began to leak out.
But the vastness of the Brazilian jungle and the lack of
transportation made investigation difficult.

By 1912 the rubber merchants realized they had
pushed the advantage of their monopoly too far. An
enterprising Englishman named Wickham had smuggled
thousands of rubber seedlings out of Brazil. These he
planted in the Malay Peninsula, where they flourished.
Labor was plentiful in the Far East, and it was much
easier to collect latex from orderly rows of planted trees
than from the haphazard growth of the Brazilian jungle.
Also, plantations near Singapore and Colombo were
close to well-established steamer routes. In Brazil

freighters had to travel hundreds of miles up the Amazon to collect the rubber.

In 1912, 88 percent of the world's rubber had been coming from Brazil. Three years later that percentage had dropped to 42. In dismay, the Brazilian rubber growers realized their day of glory was over. The opera house closed its doors. The fine mansions fell into decay. By 1923, the Brazilian jungle supplied only 8 percent of the world's total rubber supply. Today it is even less.

But the Indians who went back to their jungle clearings never forgot the treatment they had received and never forgave the overlords. Around the evening fires, stories of the cruelties were repeated. Even recently such Indians as the wild Chavantes might shoot an outsider on sight.

3

WILD LIFE OF THE BRAZILIAN JUNGLE

Like the plant life of the Rain Forest, the animal life exists on clear-cut levels.

In the topmost branches of the trees live the parrots, macaws, and a score of other birds. Lower down are the tanagers, finches, warblers. Among the lowest branches, the heavier birds are found: curassows, umbrella birds, and ivory-billed woodpeckers. Upon the ground itself are land rails, bitterns, tinamous.

Four-footed animals also have their special zones. In the treetops, monkeys and squirrels. On the second level, sloths, opossums, long-tailed porcupines. Among the lower branches, coatis, kinkajous, and smaller cats.

On ground level, the jaguars and pumas, peccaries and tapirs, anteaters and armadillos.

As elsewhere in the Rain Forest, there are many giant forms of life. The capybara, belonging to the rodent family, is as big as a sheep and weighs a hundred pounds. There is a spider large enough to catch birds. The red grasshopper is the size of a sparrow. Tucandeiro ants are over two inches long, and their bite can produce a fever which may be fatal.

From its nose to the tip of its tail, the giant anteater

The giant anteater is seven feet long.

of the Rain Forest is seven feet long. Standing erect, it is taller than a tall man. Its front feet are armed with powerful curving claws that can slice through the clay of an anthill as easily as if it were butter. The animal's mouth is little more than a small hole in the end of its snout. From this darts a two-foot tongue that forages like lightning among the exposed ants. When angered, the anteater becomes a bitter enemy. It has been known to kill a jaguar by crushing the larger animal in its powerful arms, and slashing with its claws.

The closest relative of this jungle giant is the silky anteater. This little creature has a body only six inches long. It swings from branch to branch, using its tail almost like an extra hand.

The tapir is one of the most astonishing animals in the Rain Forest. Weighing hundreds of pounds, its body resembles that of a pig. It has a short, elephant-like snout and small near-sighted eyes. It has a mane like that of a horse. There are three toes on its forefeet and four on its hind feet. A vegetarian, the tapir feeds on the rich plants that line rivers and lakes. The fresh meat of this strange animal is the tenderest and best flavored of all the creatures of the jungle.

The tapir feeds on water plants and grasses.

The Brazilian Jungle

The jaguars and pumas of the Brazilian Rain Forest are the largest of their kind. Unlike most members of the cat family, jaguars seem actually to enjoy the water. In the shallows of the river, they catch fish, a favorite food of theirs. Although bold and ruthless hunters, they seldom attack a man unless provoked.

Three things which the dwellers of the jungle greatly fear are the great black wasps, the marching armies of soldier ants, and the huge herds of white-lipped peccaries. The last are by far the most dangerous for any creature caught off guard.

Peccaries are lean, blackish-gray, razor-backed, with curved tusks. Indeed they look much like ordinary half-wild pigs until they move. The charge of a herd is a thunder of hoofs, a rattling of tusks, a welter of uplifted snouts, a sea of red eyes.

In the Rain Forest there are many monkeys. Unlike those of Africa and Asia, they can hang by their tails. This ability is not limited to monkeys. Rain Forest porcupines, tree-climbing anteaters, and the raccoon-like kinkajou also have tails they can use for grasping.

The cebus is probably the most familiar monkey, because it is the kind used by organ grinders. These little gray animals are the prettiest and most friendly of all the species in the forest.

The star acrobat of the jungle is the spider monkey. Using the ropelike lianas as a trapeze, he will launch himself through fifty feet of space, to catch hold of a bough where he has spied some tidbit to his liking.

Monkeys of all kinds are favorite foods of the Indians. They shoot monkeys with arrows tipped with a poison that kills the animal but does not harm the people who eat the meat.

The favorite food of all is the red howler monkey. The howler is the noisiest creature of the jungle. A hollow shell of bone in the upper part of his windpipe enables him to produce an unearthly din of noise. The commotion he produces sets all the jungle creatures to screeching, screaming, or roaring. When heard for the first time at night in the jungle, the howler's bellow sounds almost as if a score of jaguars were locked in mortal combat. Yet the animal that makes all this noise weighs only thirty pounds.

One of the most helpless creatures of the jungle is the sloth. It has no defense, for it cannot fight or flee. Instead, it hangs upside down from the bough of a tree and remains motionless for hours at a time. Its long hair

A crocodile can move with amazing speed.

is so encrusted with algae that it looks like moss. And the beast looks almost like part of the tree itself.

The crocodiles of the rivers of the Brazilian jungle are unpredictable creatures. As one suns himself on a sandspit, he looks like a log of weathered driftwood. But that log can come to life with amazing speed. Sometimes this huge reptile is cowardly and takes to the water at sight of man. But a bull crocodile which is guarding a nestful of eggs left by his mate will savagely attack anything or anyone.

Indians have a special way of killing this animal: they wrap sharp slivers of bamboo in several layers of fish intestines, and leave the bait on the river's edge at night. The crocodile gulps the bait. As soon as the fish disintegrates, the bamboo slivers pierce the internal organs of the crocodile, causing his death. The big yellow-green monsters of the Brazilian jungle weigh about a hundred pounds to each foot of length. Their close relatives, the caymans, are huge black animals.

Some of the creatures of the river are just as big as those of the land. The piarucu, one of the largest fresh-water fish in the world, may be eighteen feet long and weigh hundreds of pounds. Even the ordinary catfish is nine feet long in the Brazilian jungle.

Of all river creatures in the jungle, the piranha is the most dangerous. Although it is only a foot long, this fish has a jaw like that of a bulldog and a mouth lined with large razor-sharp teeth. It attacks man or beast without cause. One bite of its jaws can remove a circular piece of flesh as big as a silver dollar. These fish seldom attack singly, but usually in schools of hundreds or even thousands. The smell of blood drives the fish into a frenzy. A 600-pound tapir, overtaken while swimming across a river, may be reduced to a skeleton within a matter of minutes. No living thing can withstand the attack of these truly terrible fish.

Another unusual dweller of river and lake is the electric eel. In the whole animal kingdom, no more than half a dozen creatures can produce an electric charge, and these are all fish. Of these the electric eel discharges by far the strongest current—several hundred volts. Unlike other electric fish, the eel can control the discharge of electricity. It uses its current to kill or paralyze its prey. It locates its victim by sending out weak electric charges. These are reflected back to it much as radar picks up distant objects. Its dull greenish-gray body is four or five feet long.

Even more to be feared than the electric eel is the giant anaconda. This member of the boa family is the world's largest snake. Usually it is 25 to 30 feet long, or even more. The anaconda's skin is a sort of greenish-black. It has a row of powerful teeth on either side of the jaws, slightly curved and sloping toward the throat. It is quick-tempered and vicious. Although it is a water snake, it lives chiefly on land mammals.

The land boa is a much less threatening creature. In fact, Indians sometimes tame land boas and use them as household pets to catch mice and rats. Indians call the boa the "deer-swallower," because deer are one of the creature's favorite foods. The boa, incidentally, makes excellent eating, for its tender white meat tastes somewhat like chicken.

There are many other snakes in the jungle too. Among the most dangerous are the fer-de-lance, the coral snake, and the deadly bushmaster.

The lizard family also is well represented. Anyone accustomed to the harmless little lizards of North America is apt to be astonished at the jungle's 5-foot

Lizards and snakes abound in the jungle.

iguana, and by the 3-foot basilisk that seems to walk upright.

The fruit bat has a wingspan of three feet. For many years it was thought to be the dreaded vampire bat. But the vampire, which sleeps in dark places throughout the day, has a wingspan of only eight or nine inches. The vampire does not suck blood, but laps it up as a cat laps milk. It is able to cut a circular hole in the flesh without its victim being aware of the fact. Cattlemen lose more cattle to vampires than to jaguars. Often the

Toucans are colorful and noisy.

little vampire is infected with a form of rabies that is fatal to man or animal.

High above the canopy of the jungle, eagles and brown vultures wheel and glide endlessly. But the birds that really give character to the Rain Forest are the noisy jungle birds of vivid colors. These include squawking parties of parrots flapping through the trees, the toucans flying from one fruit tree to another, and the long-tailed macaws that often travel in noisy groups. Some macaws are blue and gold, others a bright scarlet. Their feathers are highly prized by the Indians.

In the shallows of pond or river wade lovely pink spoonbills. And storks stand five feet high, with white bodies, slim black legs, black heads and beaks, and dull ruby throats.

Some jungle birds have very distinctive songs. The anvil bird strikes a chiming note as clear and beautiful as any sound that can be heard in nature. The flautero has a lilting song that is like a delicate flute. The tinamou's song runs nimbly up and down the scale. But the bell bird's note sounds like the tolling of a funeral bell.

The insects of the jungle have been responsible for

more deaths than all the jaguars, crocodiles, and poisonous snakes put together.

The dank Rain Forest is an insect paradise, for the rays of the sun seldom penetrate below the treetops. The number and variety of Rain Forest insects passes belief.

The mosquito alone has been one of the chief obstacles to the conquest of the jungle. It has ruined engineering and farming projects, the construction of roads and settlements. The anopheles mosquito, carrier of malaria, is the greatest killer. It is estimated that more than 100,000,000 people throughout the world suffer from this disease.

The little aëdes mosquito carries yellow fever. Great cities such as Rio de Janeiro are free of these pests. But in the jungle they are still a threat.

In the jungle there are ants of every description. Some are very dangerous; others are not. The sauba, or leaf-cutting ants, are the plague of the Indians' gardens. Saubas travel in columns, each ant holding aloft a piece of leaf, like an umbrella. They can devastate an entire garden within a single night.

But perhaps the most astonishing of all are the army or soldier ants. They have this name because they move

Spoonbills wade in the shallows.

in marching order, with leaders stationed like officers at regular intervals, apparently giving orders from every side. They look like mobilized armies, millions strong. Soldier ants might take over your camp site and leave it as free from dirt as a Dutch kitchen. There won't be a speck of grease left anywhere. Your cooking utensils will be as shiny as if they had just been scoured. The bones of the wild turkey you had for dinner will be as clean-picked and polished as those of a museum specimen.

The Brazilian Jungle

There are numerous wasps in the Rain Forest, all poisonous to some degree. The most exasperating is the small stingless bee, sometimes called the "sweat bee." These pests attach themselves by the hundreds to every inch of exposed, sweaty flesh. They crawl into a man's ears, his eyes and nose, his gaping mouth, his clothing. These small yellow-brown demons can make life in the jungle a misery.

Another plague of the jungle is the tick or carapato. Leaves become covered with ticks which brush off on passers-by. Then each one buries its head under the victim's skin and inflates itself with blood. Extreme caution must be used in removing the tick so that its body does not break off. When this happens, the jaws are left embedded in a man's suffering flesh.

But the jungle, in spite of dangers and discomforts, weaves a spell about a man who lives there for long. Somehow, he generally wants to return.

4

MAN
AGAINST
THE JUNGLE
IN BRAZIL

For many centuries, Indians have managed to live and raise their families in the hostile Rain Forest of Brazil. For the most part, they live on the edge of the jungle, dwelling along the rivers and streams, hunting and fishing for food. For traveling through the jungle, they may widen paths already made by wild animals. But they prefer the easier method of using their long dugout canoes.

Yet in spite of this over-all pattern, there is great variety in the customs of the many tribes. This is seen in their manner of preparing and wearing clothing. One tribe makes a fine cloth, the women spinning cotton,

Many jungle dwellers travel by dugout canoe.

the men weaving it. Other tribes use the cloth-like inner bark of certain trees. Still others use feathers of parrots, egrets, or macaws. Some tribes rely almost entirely on tattooing as a form of covering. But more remote dwellers of the Rain Forest wear no clothing in any form. You would expect that jungle insects would make life miserable for them. But Indians know which plants are insect repellents. And they may have built up a kind of immunity.

The houses of the Indians vary almost as much as

their clothing. One of the most interesting dwellings is the malocca in which thirty or forty families live, eat, and sleep together.

Made of bamboo, a malocca may be more than a hundred feet long and as much as eighty feet wide. Often it is raised above the ground on posts as a protection against floods and reptiles. The roof is thatched, with an overhang that sweeps almost to the ground. A small opening at each end admits light and forms both entrance and exit. There are no windows.

Generally a malocca is a model of cleanliness. Hammocks are slung from the posts that support the roof. Bows and arrows, spears, blowguns, and clubs are hung neatly along the walls.

Along each side of this single great room, cook fires glow in shallow clay bowls. Each fire belongs to a different family. The fires are kept burning all night long as a way of scaring off the ghosts that are supposed to fill the darkness. But since jungle nights are damp and cold and the people own no coverings of any sort, a night without fire would be miserable indeed. Every few hours throughout the night, some member of a family replenishes the fire.

The Brazilian Jungle

Two hours before sunrise, the cold has reached its height. Then the jungle dwellers take to the river because the water is warmer than the air. This bath sustains them until breakfast. By noon they are in the river again, this time to cool off from the heat. By late afternoon they plunge in once more, just for the fun of it. Sometimes crocodiles and piranhas manage to spoil the fun, but not for long.

The dweller of the Rain Forest puts in many hours of work each day. Life in the jungles of South America is not easy. Birds and monkeys raid the gardens and gobble up fruits and nuts long before they are ripe. Hunters must seek out their game with painstaking care. While the men are hunting in the jungle, women spend most of their days preparing food and tending the gardens.

The chief food of the Indians is manioc. It means as much to them as bread to an American, oatmeal to a Scot, or potatoes to an Irishman. The tuber from which manioc is made is highly poisonous, but long ago Indians learned to remove the poison and produce a nourishing flour. After the juices have been squeezed and washed out, manioc is pounded to the consistency of sawdust. Then it is made into cakes. Heating removes the final poisons. Manioc is a practical food because it can be easily carried.

Do not imagine, however, that a jungle dinner is entirely tasteless. On occasion you may sit down to a meal of roast venison or duckling, corn on the cob, sweet yams baked in the embers, even a dessert made of peanuts and wild honey.

Some Indian foods are surprising to say the least. Toasted termites are considered a delicacy. Caterpillars and grubs of various kinds find their way to the dinner

Hunters seek game for meat.

table. Turtle eggs are favorite tidbits; the Indian simply punctures the rubbery skin of the egg and pops the contents into his mouth.

Even in the jungle, which teems with wild life, it is not easy to hunt meat for the table. For every forest creature has some means of self-protection. Some are well camouflaged. Others have unusually good scent or hearing. Others move like lightning.

Bows and arrows are often used for fishing. Yet it is difficult to learn to fish by bow and arrow because

Some Indians fish with bows and arrows.

things under water often appear to be slightly out of line.

The jungle hunter's 7-foot bow is made of black palmwood. It is a beautiful weapon that only a strong man can bend. Sometimes the hunter uses a 12-foot blowgun. This is a hollow tube of wild cane cemented in a case of bamboo. The inside of the tube is about half an inch in diameter. The darts are made from the center ribs of palm leaves, twelve inches long and less than one-sixteenth of an inch thick. They are as sharp as needles and tipped with poison. The hunter sets the blowgun to his lips and gives a single puff. The dart speeds toward its victim.

Curare poison is black and thick. The hunter carries it in a small gourd slung around his neck. The making of curare is a secret, often known only to the witch doctor. It is said to contain the juice of the strychnos plant, along with big black tucandeira ants, little red fire ants, a scorpion or two, and the crushed fangs of the lethal bushmaster.

The tribe's witch doctor cures illness and performs magic to produce rain or drought. He interprets dreams and instructs a man how to evade enemies, both seen and unseen. For all his hocus-pocus, the witch doctor is the real teacher of the tribe. Usually he is more clever and observant than his fellows. He has a truly impressive knowledge of jungle medicines. He knows how to set broken bones and perform crude surgery. From careful observation of the movements of insects, birds, and animals, he can predict the weather with amazing accuracy.

Most outsiders have found the Indians to be exceptionally honest. The scientist or explorer, with his trade goods and personal possessions, seldom finds an article missing. If a stranger in an Indian village follows the local customs, he is well received, well fed, and well cared for when he is ill.

Four centuries ago, the bullets and diseases of the first Spanish conquerors brought suffering and death to the Indians. Today, through the wise policy of the Brazil's Indian Protective Service, the Indians of the jungle are once more coming into their own.

In fact, the jungle country of Brazil is undergoing a great change. A full-scale program of health education, sponsored by the Brazilian government, is reaching out into the remotest settlements. Huge drainage projects are being undertaken. DDT has worked miracles in areas which for years have suffered from malaria. War

Man Against the Jungle in Brazil

Planes today fly over the wildest parts of the jungle.

is being carried on against such diseases as hookworm, dysentery, and typhus.

The back country is being made livable for creatures other than crocodiles and boa constrictors. Thousands of hardy pioneers are leaving the coastal cities to try their luck in the interior.

For many years the air route from North America to Rio followed the coastal bulge of Brazil. Airlines didn't dare fly the straight route over the jungle. A plane forced down might not be rescued.

The Brazilian Jungle

Now, with larger planes that carry more fuel, the main line of travel is straight from Caracas over the jungle to Rio de Janeiro. This route cuts 1500 miles off the old course that followed the coast. Part of the new route passes over the country of the savage Chavantes, who still remember the cruelties of the rubber hunters.

Since emergency landing fields had to be built in that territory, the friendship of the Chavantes had to be won. At first the Indians shot their arrows at low-flying planes. The pilots returned the fire by dropping gifts— food, knives, and cloth. Gradually hostility was broken down. In some cases the Chavantes even helped to build the airstrips.

There have been many developments in the Brazilian jungle. But the jungle is so dense that it still looks, from the air, like a mighty sea of green. Rivers that empty into the Amazon look like tiny ribbons. Only an occasional small break in the green expanse shows where a town has sprung up along the air route.

THE INDONESIAN JUNGLE

5

THE JUNGLE ISLANDS

The Malay Peninsula, in southeast Asia, has the hottest and dampest climate in the world. It is covered with a maze of vegetation even denser than that of the Brazilian jungle. Malaya is perhaps the most ancient of the world's jungle regions.

Off the Malayan coast lies the largest group of islands anywhere. They make up Indonesia, sometimes called the East Indies. To early American sea captains they were known also as the Spice Islands. From their shores the fragrance of cinnamon and cloves drifted far out to sea.

There are four major islands in this group—Java, Sumatra, Borneo, and Celebes. From the western point of Sumatra to the eastern borders of New Guinea, they

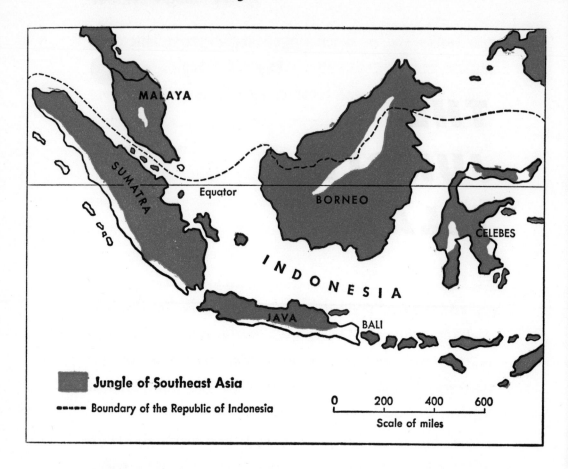

Jungle of Southeast Asia

----- Boundary of the Republic of Indonesia

0   200   400   600

Scale of miles

stretch for 4000 miles along the equator. In fact, the equator divides each of the two largest islands, Sumatra and Borneo, into almost equal parts.

Much of the area is, of course, water; but the total land mass of these jungle islands is 750,000 square miles. This is roughly the size of the United States east of the Mississippi River.

Unlike the level plateau of Brazil, the mountains of

the Indies rise in sheer jagged angles from mile-deep chasms in the ocean floor. Here is a region of great volcanic activity, the most dangerous earthquake zone in the world. There are well over two hundred active volcanoes in Indonesia. The volcanoes of Indonesia have helped produce a soil of great richness. Such soil is well supplied with lime, magnesia, iron, potash, and phosphoric acid.

Since almost no seasonal change occurs in Indonesia, vegetation flourishes the year around. Steady winds, called monsoons, blow from the southwest in summer, from the northeast in winter. Their pressure is so moderate that all foliage seems to stand still, as if holding its breath in the heat before bursting dramatically into bloom. In fact, what we would call a breeze in America is practically unknown in most of Indonesia.

Because the East Indies lie between Asia and Australia, they show the influence of both great land masses. They contain plants and animals common in Asia and Australia. This is because the islands have been connected to the mainland at various times. Over the ages the sea level has risen and fallen, and the jungle islands have been joined together and then separated. The connection between Asia and Australia has been broken, re-established, and broken again.

The Indonesian Jungle

A newcomer in Indonesia soon classifies the climate as warm, hot, hotter, hottest. For a stranger, the humidity along the seacoast is almost unbearable. An ordinary hot day along the coast can find the thermometer standing at 120° Fahrenheit. But the heat decreases as you climb the mountains.

Malaya and the Indies have the greatest and most regular rainfall in the world. This rainfall increases with the altitude. On Mt. Singgalang, near the equator in Sumatra, it rained 320 days in one year. The humidity averaged 93 percent. Nearly every night a fine drizzle falls upon the upland jungle. Usually the sky clears in the morning, but it becomes overcast in the afternoon. The hot moist air and the almost continuous vapor bath are just right for the densest jungle growth.

6

PLANTS OF THE INDONESIAN JUNGLE

The mangrove tree, propped up on its stilt-like roots, is typical of the vegetation along the coast. It grows in thick, matted belts. It is a curious plant, like a small-leafed laurel with its feet in the water. It flourishes best in soil that is flooded by the tides. The seedlings develop on the tree itself and drop like darts into the black mud. There they send out roots within a matter of hours. The wood of the tree looks like a rich, dark-red mahogany and has a handsome grain. For centuries Malayans have used mangrove wood to make charcoal for their cook fires.

In the midst of the densest mangrove swamps, the

Pandanus fruit is edible, and its leaves have many uses.

nipa palm is sure to be found. This is a deep-rooted tree. Its light green leaves stand out in contrast to the darkness of the swamp growth. The stem is so short that the leaves seem to grow out of the ooze. From this tree the natives make baskets, household objects, and roofing for their houses.

The jungle of Indonesia extends from a strip of vegetation along the coast to a height of 5000 feet above sea level. In the foothills of the mountains we see rattan palms for the first time. Over them climb vines that may be more than 220 yards long, with spikes that stand up like lightning rods. During their flowering season these lianas add a few bright spots of color to the usual green. Most blossoms in the jungle are invisible from the ground, since they open in the light above the foliage.

Even orchids here are small and dull. None of the wild fruit here is comparable in taste to such fruits as raspberries and strawberries in the temperate zones. The intense heat and eternal damp seem to drain flavor and fragrance out of fruit and flower.

Here and there you will see magnificent groups of the valuable camphor tree. Now and again you will discover the famous warangin, a tree sacred to the native peoples of the East. The most celebrated single warangin grows in the island of Bali, where it covers more than an acre and a half.

At least 150 species of palm trees are found in Indonesia. One of the most useful is the sago palm. Its soft inner part provides the natives (especially of New Guinea) with their principal food.

Bamboo—splendid groves of it—stand as high as 130 feet. The leaves range from a bright green to a dull yellow. This "grass tree" loves light, and in search of it climbs the steepest slopes, most notably in the mountains of Sumatra. Bamboo takes enormous quantities of water from the soil and grows very rapidly. The uses of this fabulous grass tree are many. It forms the framework, the floor, and the walls of native houses. Sections of it are used as water pipes or containers for food. Clever workmen turn it into birdcages of fantastic design. It can be used for rafts large enough to transport an entire family; or tiny splinters of it can be fashioned into needle-like darts. Of all the trees of the Indies, bamboo is perhaps the most important.

As the lowland jungle climbs steadily up the mountainsides, certain tree families give way to others. Some species of cone-bearing trees reach a height of two hundred feet. In Sumatra and Borneo they make up more than 50 percent of the upland jungle. These trees first came from the Himalaya Mountains. They advanced into the East Indies, where they mingled with the casuarinas of Australia.

On the lower slopes of western Indonesia, the forest also contains the curious pitcher plant, with leaves that close up like big, lidded urns. As you climb higher and higher, flowering plants become more numerous. Many of the flowers, such as buttercups and scentless violets,

Indonesian houses are often made of bamboo.

are similar to flowers that grow in the temperate zones.

The greatest teak forests of Indonesia are found in Java. Some people believe that this valuable tree was brought from Indochina to Java by Indian colonists. For over half a century, the wild teak trees have been cut down. But new trees have been planted in their place. In appearance, however, teak forests are open and monotonous, with few vines, insects, or birds.

One of the most astonishing trees of the Indonesian forest is the so-called "strangler fig." Its seeds begin to grow on tall trees far above the ground. The seedling rapidly becomes a stout bush which sends roots down through the air. Some of these cling to the trunk of the host tree. Others reach out into the air. Eventually the roots reach the soil and take firm hold. There they multiply, until the trunk of the supporting tree is surrounded by a powerful, woody network. The crown of the fig, meanwhile, has become large and heavy. After a time the host tree dies, literally strangled to death by its own seedlings. This leaves the "strangler fig" as a hollow tree in its own right. It is often very large and may reach the highest growth level of the Indonesian jungle.

One of the products of the Indonesian jungle seems to have a bright future: kapok. Kapok trees grow to be as high as a hundred feet, their branches extending awkwardly at right angles to their trunk. These trees of the Indies produce nine-tenths of the world's supply of kapok. The pods are harvested just before they are ready to burst. The silky fibers are separated from the little black seeds by hand. Kapok is sound-absorbent and water-resistant. When floated, it supports thirty times its weight. It is used for insulation and for the stuffing of pillows.

7

WILD ANIMALS OF INDONESIA

Wild animals of the jungle islands are exciting and varied. There are gorgeous peacocks and other songless birds of exotic plumage. There are more than a hundred different kinds of snakes, including the king cobra, the python, and the dreaded krait. There are honey bears and the elusive Malayan antelope. The rhinoceros—native to Java, Borneo, and Sumatra—is similar to the one-horned variety of India. The delightful little mouse-deer, standing only one foot high, is important in native folklore.

Tigers are common in western Java, as well as in Bali and Sumatra. They are powerful animals. Their spring is quick, and they can deal a shattering blow with their forepaws. Their tawny hide, striped with black, is wonderful camouflage for the kind of vegetation in which they prefer to hide. Usually their prey is wild game, such as deer.

When a tiger becomes fat and lazy, he likes to settle down in some spot where beef and water are easily available. Here he establishes a truce with the villages, killing a bullock or a cow once in every five or six days. He does not spring upon the back of his victim, as does the leopard. Rather he springs for the forequarters of his prey, seizing the throat from underneath. He will often consume fifty or sixty pounds of meat the first night. After that, the tiger eats whenever he wishes, by day or night, until the whole carcass is finished.

Occasionally a tiger will become a man eater. Often these night prowlers terrify the inland villages. They claim many victims before the terrified people band together to hunt them down. The average size of a full-grown tiger is some nine feet from nose to tail tip. Its weight is from 275 to 325 pounds.

The black Malayan leopard is a more terrifying enemy than the tiger. The leopard conceals itself along the limbs of trees and springs without warning as its

The Malayan leopard is a terrifying enemy.

victim passes beneath. Its claws and teeth can inflict more damage than a tiger's.

Natives have a novel way of hunting these big cats. They use birdlime, which is a sort of glue made from the gum of a tree. The hunter spreads the birdlime along the trail to the water hole and covers it lightly with leaves. The moment the leopard puts his feet into the gluey substance, he becomes enraged and helpless. Frantically the leopard tries to lick or bite the glue off his feet. He merely gets it smeared over his face and plastered over his eyes. He sits down and howls with exasperation. At that point the hunter dashes in with his spear and puts an end to his old enemy. Birds and monkeys also are easily captured by artful spreading of birdlime.

Another beautiful animal of the cat family is the clouded leopard. Its name comes from its grayish-brown fur, with its long, irregular spots. Malayans have a name of their own for this splendid creature: *Rimau-dahan*, which means Tiger-of-the-Trees. Actually the clouded leopard spends most of its life in the upper branches, feeding on birds and small mammals. It only comes down to the ground to seek water. For this reason, it is not a great menace to men and their cattle.

Sometimes leopards are forced to fight the animals which natives call *Baba-rusa*—the wild black boars of the jungle. It would seem that the wily leopard would have the advantage in such a struggle, but this is not often the case. The jungle boar is unbelievably quick. Its speed, its big head and thick hide, its sharp hoofs and tusks are mighty weapons. When wild boars travel in herds, any sensible hunter gives them a wide berth.

The wild cattle called benteng are dreaded by the natives too. Their vision and sense of smell are keen.

They charge with terrific speed and without warning.

A hunter of benteng does well to keep his eye on a tree as a possible refuge. His only escape from a direct charge may be to sidestep, or to fall flat on his face and let the beast run over him. The benteng's neck is so short that its horns cannot reach a man lying flat on the ground. If a hunter hasn't been knocked unconscious by the first attack, he can jump for the tree before the benteng can check the speed of its charge. But once the man is caught on the beast's horns, no escape is possible.

There are many different kinds of monkeys in Indonesia; but the ape known as orang-utan is found only in Borneo and Sumatra. Its name is from the Malay *orang* meaning "man," and *utan*, "of the woods." This animal is second in size to the gorilla of Africa. It stands some four and a half feet tall. Its outstretched arms reach more than seven and a half feet. The power of those arms is tremendous. A fully grown orang-utan can bend a half-inch steel pipe as easily as if it were made of rubber.

This ape never travels on the ground if he can swing from tree to tree. Since there are few open spaces in the jungle, he is usually found high up in the branches. He swings for amazing distances.

The Indonesian Jungle

Orang-utans live in family groups numbering from forty to sixty. The largest and strongest ape is the chief. They make their homes on platforms of branches. Natives hunt orang-utans with blowpipes and poisoned darts. These weapons are similar to those of the Indians of the Brazilian jungle.

The strangest-looking monkey of Borneo is named the Proboscis—a word meaning "nose." Since most monkeys have almost no nose at all, the Proboscis monkey is an unusual sight. His nose is enormous, and no one has ever discovered what particular use it is to the animal.

Another and more familiar monkey is the pigtailed macaque, frequently seen in zoos. It is also found in India, Burma, the Malay Peninsula, Borneo, Sumatra, even in parts of China and Japan. It gets its name from its short, curling tail.

Some macaques have no tail at all. These animals race through the treetops, in large groups, feeding on insects, fruits, and tiny lizards. Their puffy cheeks make excellent storehouses for extra food. Some macaques are almost impossible to train as pets, for they are fierce and vicious and resist gestures of friendship.

To a stranger in the Indonesian jungle, there seem to

The pigtailed macaque has a curling tail.

be countless kinds and varieties of reptiles. In addition to snakes, crocodiles in the rivers are even more numerous and ferocious than those of the Brazilian jungle. They haunt the places where people bathe or wash their clothes, and in densely populated areas they kill hundreds of victims every year.

Usually the elephant of Malaya and Indonesia is referred to as the Indian elephant. More properly it should be called the Asiatic elephant, for its range extends from India to the Malay Peninsula and its neighboring islands.

The Indonesian Jungle

The elephants in zoos and circuses are usually of this Asiatic strain, since they are far easier to tame than their wild African cousins.

Elephants are vegetarians. In one day an elephant may consume 150 pounds of leaves and grass. And he is capable of drinking fifty gallons of water a day. He is equally at home in the densest jungle or in the grassy plains. For generations, the native rulers of various islands had these animals captured and trained. Until 1929 they were used for transportation by the Dutch East Indian Army.

The mahout, or driver, sits on the elephant's neck and presses with his knees upon the elephant's ears. Without uttering a sound, the mahout can direct his mount to go forward, to turn left or right, to pick up objects, to salute or halt. One famous scientist put the elephant third among the ten most intelligent wild animals. Only the chimpanzee and orang-utan outrank him.

Driving a herd of wild elephants into a trap is thrilling and dangerous. To make a trap, trees twenty-five feet long are dragged to the spot and planted deep in the ground. Each one is braced by smaller trees which will help to withstand the tremendous pressure of a lunging herd. The trap is almost circular. Two long wings come together near the entrance. After all the posts have been properly braced, they are lashed together with rattan ropes as strong as wire. Then the whole thing is camouflaged with leaves. When it is completed, the trap seems a part of the surrounding jungle.

If an elephant herd is located a couple of miles away, it is the hunters' job to drive the great animals into the trap. With drums and other noisemakers, men called beaters form a long line behind the herd. At first they are perfectly quiet. If the elephants suspect hunters are near, the entire herd will stampede.

Then a signal is given. Men pound their drums. The noise is deafening. Elephants lunge away to escape the uproar. The only route leads toward the concealed trap. With trunks upraised, the great beasts trumpet shrilly. The beaters herd them through the jungle. At last the elephants storm into the runways leading to the trap's entrance. When the last elephant is safely inside, the gate crashes down. There is a great din of bellowing and trumpeting.

Small holes are cut in the rattan webbing between the posts so that the baby elephants may be coaxed away from the parent herd. At birth these babies stand about three feet high and weigh some two hundred pounds. They are easily weaned in captivity. A native trainer dips the infant's trunk into a pail of warm milk, doubles up the trunk, and puts it back into the baby's mouth. The little elephant quickly catches on; soon it is feeding itself.

But the work of breaking the grown wild elephants is a more difficult matter. A single false move on the part of the trainers may mean disaster. At first the animals are given little food, because they are easier to handle when they are hungry.

In the meantime, enormous posts are driven into the ground to form V-shaped stocks. Bales of food are placed inside. One by one the hungry elephants are guided straight into the stocks. They fall on the food. Then the posts are drawn together at the top. They pin each elephant securely behind the ears. Ropes are tied around its feet and knees. The animal cannot escape.

For some time the elephant remains in the stocks. A special trainer is assigned to it. The trainer sees that the animal is well fed and rinsed at regular intervals with water. Its back is scratched. Under the kindest treatment, the animal loses its fear of man in a short time.

When the elephant will let the trainer sit on its head, it is released from the stocks. It is still strongly hobbled. At this moment a dozen men stand by to trip the elephant if it should try to bolt.

Soon it learns to kneel, to turn, to back and pull. It becomes intensely fond of its trainer. Once broken, the mighty elephant remains docile and obedient throughout a long life.

In the teak forests of Java and Burma, elephants are trained to supervise other elephants. In the big lumber

The untamed elephant is put in the stocks.

mills, these beasts roll the teak logs into position for the saws. With their heads, two elephants push the logs up inclined skids to the platform while a third elephant bosses the job. The boss elephant knows that the log must move up the skids in a certain manner, and that the two pushers must keep exact time. In his trunk the boss holds a length of chain which he uses like a whip. If one pusher slacks his effort, the boss whacks him with the chain.

Next to the trained elephant, the water buffalo, or carabao, is the major work animal of the Indies. The carabao's massive horns have a spread of six or seven feet. Its hide is thick and without pores. Since it cannot sweat, this great beast has to cool off each day by wallowing in the mud. Without this cooling mud bath, the carabao rushes about wildly, causing great damage to life and property. Well handled, these great beasts are easily managed by small boys, who care for them.

Birds swarm everywhere: the boatbill heron; the tickbird, whose white wings haunt the buffalo; the huge argus pheasant, whose rapid flight through the densest jungle makes capture almost impossible.

The insect life of this region is probably the most

The water buffalo is a work animal.

varied in the entire world. There are some 250,000 species in Malaya alone, including the gigantic beetle called *Buprestis*. As in other tropical regions, the insects are more deadly to man than the wild animals. The sluggish jungle rivers are the breeding places of disease parasites.

MEN
OF THE
JUNGLE
ISLANDS

8

Thousands of years ago, waves of people poured down from Asia, through Siam and Burma into the narrow Malay Peninsula. From there they fanned out into the scattered islands of the East Indies. Today their descendants are of many races and many languages.

More than 75,000,000 people live on the jungle islands of the Indies. Java alone has 50,000,000. It is the most densely populated area of its size in the entire world. The little island of Bali alone supports 1,000,000 people.

Physically, Indonesians are among the shortest people on earth. The men seldom stand higher than five feet,

Every blade of rice must be transplanted by hand.

and the women less than that. They are beautifully pro-
portioned, and very graceful in action or repose. Their
cheekbones are wide and their noses flat. The mouth
and lips of almost every Indonesian are stained red from
chewing betel nuts. An American once asked an elderly
Indonesian why his people stained their teeth with betel.
The old native, eying the white man's gleaming teeth,
answered calmly: "Because we do not care to look like
dogs."

Almost every Indonesian is calm. He seldom makes

a hurried movement. A harsh, loud voice is never heard. Furthermore, if he has nothing of importance to say, he remains silent. An American's constant chatter is puzzling to him.

Most Indonesians—even those who live in the densest jungle—are farmers. Rice is their chief food. The jungle dwellers clear and burn away the natural growth. With digging sticks, they plant grains of rice in the rich, moist, ash-covered soil.

Indonesians live close to the earth. With their own hands, they produce nearly everything out of what the land has to offer. They are people of the streams and the jungles and the soil. And it is very rich soil, as proved by the fact that the Javanese (packed more than 800 to the square mile) live almost entirely on the products of their own land. Fortunately, Indonesians require very little in the way of food. A bowl of rice sprinkled with a bit of dried fish and a vegetable sauce makes a meal. Two such dishes a day are sufficient for any grown man or woman.

THE AFRICAN

JUNGLE

9

JOURNEY INTO THE JUNGLE

For impressive beauty, no other region on earth matches Equatorial Africa. Snow-capped mountains, turbulent rivers, broad grassy plains, steaming Rain Forest—the Belgian Congo has them all. One half of its 904,000 square miles is jungle country. Yet in all this tremendous area there are only 13,000,000 native inhabitants, and some 100,000 Europeans. Compare this number with little Java's 50,000,000.

The Congo is a country of extremes. Native tribes, ranging from four-foot Pygmies to seven-foot Watusi giants, live in the jungle. Yet in the very heart of this country you will find modern cities of skyscrapers and

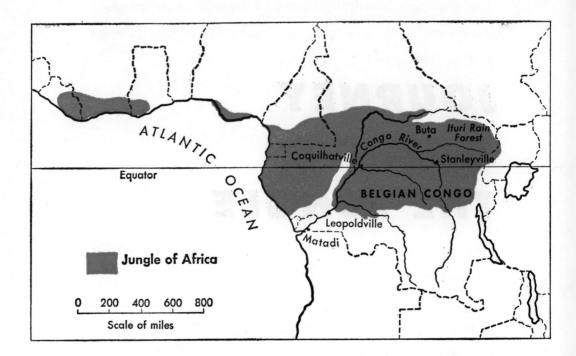

Jungle of Africa

0 200 400 600 800

Scale of miles

boulevards, of automobiles and airplanes. In the jungles
nearby, there are hundreds of thousands of wild animals.
They are hunted by warriors whose bodies are painted
and scarred according to tribal custom.

The Congo lies across the equator. Throughout the
year, the hours of daylight almost equal those of night.
The sun rises about 6 A.M. and sets about 6 P.M. Allow-
ing a half-hour for dawn and an equal time for twilight,
this means about thirteen hours of daylight each day

The Congo is hot and wet for six months, just plain hot the other six. In dry seasons the dust can choke a man or a diesel engine.

Through this land, the Congo River twists and turns for almost 3000 miles on its journey to the Atlantic Ocean. Twice it crosses the equator. This great river ranks as the fifth longest in the world. Only the Nile, the Mississippi-Missouri, the Amazon, and the Yangtze are longer. In spite of aviation and a network of roads, the Congo and its tributaries form the basis of this jungle country's communications.

At the mouth of the river, on the Atlantic shore, a trading station called "Banana" drowses in the sun. Here a traveler who wishes to venture into the heart of the continent must take one of the wood-burning river steamers. The journey requires many stops along the way to refuel, for the river's current is powerful. Thousands and thousands of cords of finest mahogany are burned yearly to stoke the boilers of these river boats.

On the lower decks of the steamer, native Africans are crowded together. All have their possessions with them—children and livestock, pet parrots and monkeys. For days they will cook and eat and sleep in that crowded space.

The African Jungle

As soon as the steamer leaves the Atlantic Ocean and enters the lower part of the river, the heat settles down. The air is stifling, breathless. Except for an occasional dark-sailed native boat, the lower Congo seems empty of life. But occasionally, as the steamer fights its way upstream, small clearings are seen on the river bank. Here traders and settlers struggle for a foothold. But almost immediately they are swallowed up by the vegetation.

On the Congo the surface of the water is as smooth as glass. But a steamer must zigzag back and forth across the river to keep in the deepest channel. In this she is guided by painted navigation markers, the only signs of civilization in this world.

All along the waterway, the bird life is remarkable. Everywhere there are cormorants, egrets, storks, and black-headed herons. A marabou is taking his mid-morning bath. Egyptian kingfishers dart down to the water's edge and return holding tiny fishes in their beaks. There are birds of prey too. One is the black-crested eagle, with enormous claws and feathered feet. Another is the chocolate-colored hawk that lives on bats. No color is more vivid than the crimson of the red-billed firefinch.

Night brings no relief from the steaming heat. The

Birds are abundant along the Congo.

The African Jungle

Southern Cross rises above the swiftly moving river. The darkness is filled with the drone of numbers of insects and the hollow *gonk-gonk* of giant African frogs.

The next day the steamer pushes on to Matadi, which lies just below the first of the great waterfalls of the Congo River. At Matadi, a railroad has been built to by-pass the rapids and carry both freight and passengers to a point farther upriver. Until the railroad was completed in 1898, there was no way at all to enter the Congo from the west.

A steamer can go upstream as far as Matadi.

The roar of the waterfalls, which are known as Livingstone's Falls, sounds like some mighty and never-ending thunderstorm. The potential power of this section of the river has been estimated at 114 million horsepower.

The engine and coaches of the Matadi railway look like something seen in an amusement park. This railroad has no mighty diesels or streamlined coaches. Old-timers in the Congo claim that the building of the 225 miles of narrow-gauge track cost the life of one native for every tie, the life of one European for every three ties. Men still discuss the cost of that project in terms of effort and human lives. Laborers were recruited from all over Africa. Food was scarce. Two years were needed to lay five miles of track through sheer rock. No wonder the astonished natives called the Belgians *Bula Matari*—breakers of rock! Before the railroad was finished, five steamboats had been carried piece by piece over that terrible road to be reassembled above the falls.

Puffing and whistling, the little engine takes curves almost at right angles, coasts down terrifying grades, crawls up others. It starts and stops with jerks.

Morning finds the tiny train jolting through scrubby country, passing one little settlement after another. At last the river widens out to form Stanley Pool, which resembles a lake fifteen miles long. And here at the station called Kinshasa the passengers take their leave of the little railway.

Kinshasa is a part of Leopoldville, which has been the capital of the Belgian Congo since 1923. This astonishing city developed in the very heart of the jungle. Only fifteen years ago it was a city of less than 40,000 people. Today its number has swelled to 265,000. No other jungle city has grown so rapidly. Helicopters spray it regularly with DDT, making mosquito nets unnecessary. The latest models of foreign and American cars throng its sixty miles of spacious streets.

The Belgian Congo is a colony of vast wealth. The Congo produces many things that make this jungle empire so important. Today it is the free world's major producer of uranium. Other important resources are diamonds, copper, cobalt, gold, palm oil, and cotton. Paper is manufactured from the unlimited supplies of jungle timber.

Ivory is often called the "white gold" of Africa. The Congo furnishes much of the ivory for the billiard balls, piano keys, knife handles, and toilet articles of the

Elephant tusks provide ivory for the world.

world. Most of the ivory now being exported is known as dead ivory. This comes from native stores accumulated through the years, or from tusks found in mysterious jungle hiding places where old elephants have gone to die. White ivory comes from the open plains; the so-called black ivory comes from the jungles. Actually it is a darkish-brown color that looks as if it had been heavily smoked. Probably this color is caused by the special type of food that the forest elephant prefers.

The African Jungle

Less than one-fifth of the ivory now being exported comes from animals recently killed. This is known as live ivory.

The traveler who pushes beyond Leopoldville into the heart of Africa finds only two more cities standing between himself and the great, mysterious Ituri Forest. These are Coquilhatville and Stanleyville.

The former lies upon the upper loop of the Congo, directly on the equator. Stanleyville—643 miles farther upriver—is one of the oldest cities in the jungle. Seventy-five years ago it was founded by Henry Stanley, the great English explorer. Here he made important treaties with the native chieftains. The four mango trees which the pioneer explorer planted on the site of the original town may still be seen.

The principal importance of the city is as the final point to which river steamers go above Leopoldville. Beyond Stanleyville, railways and roads complete a fine system of transportation.

But more than these jungle cities, it is the great Ituri Rain Forest which lures the traveler. Within its green, mysterious depths there are wild animals and native peoples unlike any others in the world.

10

THE ITURI RAIN FOREST

The road from Stanleyville to an outpost called Buta cuts like a tunnel through the lofty greenery of the forest. Along the way, native banana and manioc plantations may be seen, and occasional plantings of rice. After the first few miles, the road becomes a washboard filled with pits and ruts from the last rain.

Although the Ituri is known as a Rain Forest, it seldom rains all day or all night there. A downpour may occur for an hour or so every other day, usually around four or five o'clock each afternoon. April and November are the wettest months.

Enormous trees, bare of branches almost to the top,

tower above the lower level of vegetation. There are
many acacia trees, which look a little like huge flat-
topped parasols on lengthy handles. There are baobabs,
too, which the natives call "monkey bread." This lofty
tree has a tremendous trunk, and its thick bark protects
it well against the evaporation of the dry season. Everywhere there are magnificent mahoganies and the splendid limbali trees. Frequently the trunk of a limbali is
twenty feet across. Its wood is like that of an oak.

Elephant tracks in the road remind the traveler that
civilization has been left far behind. There are no
bridges along these jungle highways. Rivers must be
crossed on pontoons—platforms built sidewise on half
a dozen canoes.

Entering the great forest, a stranger suddenly feels
cut off from the rest of the earth. There are living, dead,
and dying trees on every side. Except where a clearing
has been burned and chopped out, a man may live his
whole life in the Ituri and never see farther than twenty
yards.

Fortunately this part of the jungle has excellent drainage, so that insect pests are not troublesome. There are
few mosquitoes. The dangerous night-feeding tick,
which carries relapsing fever, is absent here. But the

tsetse fly, carrier of sleeping sickness, is everywhere.

The tsetse has a body about one-quarter inch long. Of the thirty or more species, only four or five carry the deadly infection. Native porters always walk in single file. Each one carries a leafy branch with which to brush off any fly on the bare back of the man ahead of him. As the fly sucks its victim's blood, its body swells. When full, it begins to buzz. This tiny alarm alerts the victim, but already the damage has been done. Hundreds of thousands of natives, and many Europeans, too, have been killed by the dreaded tsetse. Travelers tell of coming to an empty village where all the inhabitants have perished of sleeping sickness.

The matted trail through the jungle makes slippery going. The traveler is lucky if he sees that rarest and shyest of African animals—the okapi. This strange beast is found only in the Ituri Forest. It is a distant relative of the giraffe, but the giraffe lives in open plains country. Under the influence of jungle conditions, the okapi differs greatly from its long-necked cousin. It is about the size of a large donkey. Its body is a rich chocolate color with a purplish tinge. The legs are striped black and white. The nose is like a snout. The males have horns—small, skin-covered, and pointed. Like the giraffe, the okapi is incapable of uttering a sound. Its meat is considered one of the great delicacies of the jungle.

In the Ituri, too, there is always a chance of coming upon a herd of elephants. The African elephant differs in many respects from its Asiatic relative. It stands higher at the shoulders, its skull is shaped more like a dome, its tusks are heavier and with out-sweeping points. But the greatest difference between the two species is in the size of the ears. Those of the African animal are enormous. When alarmed or suspicious, it flaps them back and forth like huge wings.

It is sometimes said that the Congo elephant is untamable, but this is not the fact. Since 1900, at the farm called Gangalia-no-Bodio, elephants have been trained. The training period takes up to ten years and follows a carefully worked-out plan. The company that leases out these work animals has rigid rules concerning their welfare. For example, no elephant may be put to work on a rainy morning. Every animal must be home by one o'clock, so he will have plenty of time for lunch, rest, and a bath. Since it rains almost every day in many parts of the Congo, the work elephant leads a somewhat pampered life.

The elephant's only enemy is man. Before European

hunters came into Africa, the great beast was nearly as much a creature of the plains as of the forest. Today he tends to remain within the protection of the jungle, where the risks of capture or death by bullet are not so great.

Deep in the Ituri, the little pygmy elephant is found. This is a small copy of its mammoth relative. The pygmy's ears are small and smoothly rounded, unlike those of other elephants. The first time one of these creatures was seen in captivity was in New York's Bronx Zoo. Most of the time this particular captive was docile and good-tempered. But occasionally it would indulge in a tantrum. Then its keepers kept well out of reach of the wicked little tusks. Not much is known about the life and habits of this animal since it dwells in the densest jungle in all Africa.

Next to the elephant, the hippopotamus is the largest of land animals. However, it is more at home in the water and spends most of its time there. Its huge barrel-shaped body is supported by stumpy legs. Its enormous mouth displays a great array of teeth. During the lifetime of the animal, these teeth are continually growing; but as the tips are constantly rubbing together, they stay the same length. The great beast's ears are small. The nostrils are placed upon the highest point of the muzzle. When floating in the river, the hippopotamus is able to see, hear, and breathe with only the minimum of its body exposed. When submerging, it can close its ears and nostrils to prevent the entry of water.

African natives hunt the hippopotamus during the open season by locating their prey in a part of the river that offers no hiding place. Usually the great beast will remain in one spot for hours. It allows itself to sink to the bottom, floating to the surface from time to time

A hippopotamus may weigh four tons.

to breathe. Hunters advance cautiously in their canoes. Each time the animal submerges, they move toward it.

The chief hunter prepares to cast his harpoon. This weapon has a sharp point and several yards of strong cable, to which a wooden float has been attached. When the animal shows its ears, the harpoon is driven deep between its shoulders. The hippopotamus bounds out of the water, then takes a sudden dive. The float rises to the surface. But there is no sign of the harpoon, which is stuck fast.

The victim moves under water at full speed. Excitedly the hunters follow the direction of the float. Suddenly the animal slows down. The float halts. The beast is coming up. Two more harpoons are plunged into the animal before it has time to breathe.

Now the weakened beast, bleeding from these wounds, turns to attack its tormentors. The water is churned to a fury. But the hunters are too quick. Skillfully they avoid the charges of the enraged animal and drive home the finishing blow. There will be a great feast in the village that night.

A fairly recent jungle discovery is the pygmy hippopotamus. Some years ago, three of them were captured and taken to the Bronz Zoo. Until that time, no one except native Africans knew that these remarkable little creatures existed. When fully grown, the pygmy hippopotamus weighs only three hundred pounds. Its larger relative weighs up to four tons.

The giant forest hog is another animal unknown to the outside world until fairly recent times. It ranges from British East Africa to the Belgian Congo. It has even been found as high as 10,000 feet up the slopes of Mount Kenya. A powerful beast, with heavy black bristles, it is almost six feet long. Its huge, up-curving tusks make it a dangerous foe. Forest hogs travel in bands, wearing trails through the densest undergrowth. Only the most fearless hunters dare to attack them with spears.

African lions are not jungle animals. They live and hunt only in open plains country. But the leopard is at home on the plains, in the rocky hills, and deep in the jungle. Unlike the lion, it is a solitary beast, seldom traveling in company. The African leopard seems really to be a cat with nine lives. A wounded leopard will fight to a finish, no matter how many chances he has to escape. The coloring of a leopard is distinct and conspicuous when seen in a cage. Yet it blends so well with the animal's natural surroundings that he is hardly seen. Leopards prefer to eat monkeys, baboons, and small antelopes. However, they do not object to the taste of man.

The African buffalo is one of the most dangerous of big-game animals. This is true of both the small red buffalo of the jungle and the larger black buffalo of the plains. In charging and killing a hunter, the buffalo will not turn aside while any life remains in its victim.

Perhaps the most interesting of all animals of this region is the gorilla. This huge, manlike ape lives in the lowland jungles of the Congo and the eastern borders of the mountain country. Human beings are no match for the strength of these great apes when they are fully grown.

The gorilla's face has little forehead, overhanging brows, and close-set red eyes. The nose is flat, with large nostrils. The huge head seems to fit without a neck right between the massive shoulders. The animal has a barrel-shaped chest, a tremendous length of arm, and stubby but powerful legs.

The gorilla looks fierce and savage. But it never attacks other animals to eat them. It lives on leaves and berries and roots. It will not attack a man except when

The powerful gorilla is usually shy and gentle.

irritated or protecting its young. The gorilla is a shy animal. When angered or frightened, it thumps its mighty chest. The sound carries for considerable distance like a strange drumbeat. Although it can stand upright like a man, this ape travels on all fours, and in family groups. Gorillas build no shelters. They construct sleeping places by hollowing out a circle in the ground and lining it with soft leaves.

Next to the gorilla, the chimpanzee is the most fascinating of the apes. It is found only in the jungles of Central Africa. Among the most intelligent of all animals, the chimpanzee is often seen in circuses, riding bicycles, playing ball, performing acrobatic feats. Indeed, it does many things with a skill that is strangely human. The average adult animal weighs around 150 pounds and stands five feet high. There is great strength in its long arms and powerful hands, but these apes are easily tamed and become affectionate pets. Like gorillas, chimpanzees travel in groups in their native jungles. Unlike gorillas, they build sleeping platforms in the trees. Chimpanzees have often been used by scientists experimenting in the study and cure of human diseases.

Many different kinds of monkeys live in the Ituri Forest. The most familiar are the guenons. There are

The guenon is a delightful little monkey.

over seventy varieties of this delightful little animal. The guenon's long, slim tail is useless for grasping, but its fingers are strong and wiry. It is as full of pranks as a playful puppy. Sometimes guenons are seen on the streets of Stanleyville, with native keepers who have trained them to beg for coins. These monkeys live in large groups. They travel high up in the trees under the leadership of an elderly guenon, who behaves like a stern parent.

Possibly the prettiest of all African tree dwellers is

the guereza. This medium-sized monkey is noted for its long, shiny black hair. Down its back flows a capelike mantle of pure white hair. African warriors use the fur of the guereza to make impressive headdresses. Not so many years ago, this same fur was fashionable in America as trimming for ladies' hats and dresses. Of all monkeys, guerezas make the most endearing pets. This is because of their handsome appearance and good manners.

Like most tropical regions, the African jungle has many poisonous snakes. Outstanding is the puff adder —a slow, thick-bodied reptile. It comes out of hiding usually at sunset. A man bitten by a puff adder has been known to die within twenty minutes. Unlike most snakes, this one lays no eggs and gives birth to living young.

The black mamba is greatly feared by native Africans. This slender snake belongs to the cobra family. Although black when old, it is greenish when young. Among the leaves it is almost invisible when coiled around the branch of a tree.

Another dangerous snake is the gaboon viper. Its body is as thick as a man's arm, its head is as big as his fist. It is strikingly marked with red and blue spots.

The African Jungle

This member of the adder family possesses a combination of poisons that kills its victim by paralyzing the nervous system and destroying the red cells.

The so-called "spitting snake" can eject its poison for a distance of several feet. This venom does no harm on a person's skin. But if it reaches the eye it sets up an acute inflammation which may result in blindness. This creature is a member of the cobra family.

Another snake to watch out for is the horned viper. It is scarcely more than three feet long. Its name comes from two hard, scaly growths which stand out like horns on the front of its flat, three-cornered head. Generally the horned viper is found near water, for it is an excellent swimmer. Against a background of rotting vegetation, this snake is very difficult to see. When it is alarmed or disturbed, it strikes with amazing speed.

Fortunately a man can live a long time in the African jungle without encountering any of these deadly snakes. Most of them flee from men.

PYGMIES
AND
GIANTS

Many different tribes of people live in the Ituri Rain Forest, but the Pygmies are the most unusual. Bands of Pygmies, known as Tiki-Tikis, are scattered throughout the Ituri. The men average little over four feet in height, weighing perhaps eighty pounds. The women are much slighter, and a Pygmy baby at birth is unbelievably tiny.

These people are perfectly formed little men and women. Some scientists believe they are descended from the original inhabitants of Africa. Unlike their African neighbors, they have skin of a coppery tone, similar to that of the American Indians.

The African Jungle

The Tiki-Tikis are cheerful, courageous, roving hunters. They seldom sleep in one camp for more than a few days. They plant and cultivate nothing. Many Pygmies today are practically slaves of other Africans, who push them back into the jungle and employ them as hunters.

It is an exciting experience to enter a Pygmy encampment for the first time. Word must be sent ahead by some friendly native or trader that you expect to arrive for a visit. Otherwise the whole tribe will vanish into the depths of the jungle long before you have come within hailing distance.

It takes sharp eyes to discover the Pygmies' almost hidden path as it twists and turns through a mass of ferns and creepers, for the path is only as wide as a small man's foot. No sound breaks the utter stillness in this part of the Ituri Forest. If human beings of any size live within the hollow green silence, there is no sign of them.

Here a stranger must walk carefully. What appears to be a twisted branch may prove to be a deadly snake. And a spotted-gold patch of sunlight may turn out to be a pouncing leopard. The Pygmy settlement itself comes as a surprise. The leafy shelters that pass for "houses" are scarcely three feet high. They look so much like the surrounding undergrowth that they might easily be passed by. They contain no furnishings of any sort. The beds are only plantain leaves spread upon the earth floor. There are no cooking pots. Food is eaten raw or smoked. The only possessions of these little jungle people are their bows and arrows and spears. When the tribe moves on to a new camp, there is nothing to carry except babies too small to walk.

These little men are almost as expert in the treetops as the monkeys. Often they travel considerable distances through the branches without descending to the ground. Because of the danger from crocodiles, Pygmies are afraid of the water and seldom learn to swim. Hence they have become expert bridge builders, using lianas and vines in place of ropes or cables. Building a bridge of vines is dangerous work that takes great skill.

Of all jungle people, Pygmies are the most expert hunters and the finest trackers. The Belgian government does not allow them to carry modern firearms. So they must catch their meat and defend themselves with their own handmade weapons. But with these their marksmanship is truly marvelous. Often they shoot three or four arrows, one after another, so rapidly that the last may leave the bow before the first has reached its mark.

Occasionally an arrow misses its goal. Then the little hunter flies into a rage, breaking his arrows and stamping on them. The arrows themselves are merely hard, straight reeds, tipped with poison. Two leaves, set at one end, steady the flight.

Pygmies have an unusual way of hunting small game. They stretch nets of stout fiber through the jungle. Then the women and children scatter in a wide semicircle and set up a great din. That drives the frightened animals into the net, where they are quickly killed by the hunters.

Even the mighty elephant can be caught by these tiny jungle people. Sometimes enormous traps are dug and cunningly concealed with branches and leaves.

One of the most surprising facts about these small men and women is their great appetite for all kinds of food. A Pygmy thinks nothing of consuming a stalk of sixty bananas at a single meal, in addition to as much meat as he can hold. Then he will lie on his hard earth bed and groan throughout the night. When morning comes, he is ready to repeat the performance. Pygmies are unusually fond of salt. Since almost none is found in the jungle, traders use bars of salt as money when dealing with the Pygmies.

The Pygmies are fearless hunters.

The African Jungle

In spite of a life that would seem unbearably hard for most of us, the Pygmies are always cheerful. In their own language—which few outsiders ever learn to speak —they call themselves "The Little People." They refer to other Africans as "The Real People."

A neighboring tribe of great interest is the Mangbetu. They are not so tall as the seven-foot Watusis, who live to the east. But they are giants compared to the Pygmies. They live on the fringe of the Ituri and are as different from the Little People as daylight differs from dark.

If you wish to visit the Mangbetus, you will find yourself following a trail so ancient that its clay seems to have been pounded into cement by generations of bare feet. Only the sharp hoofs of the forest buffalo can make an impression in its hard surface. Overhead, monkeys break off twigs and throw them down upon those who pass below.

As the trail leaves the gloomy forest, it suddenly forms a tunnel through grass higher than a tall man's head. The grass gives way finally to a place where all undergrowth has been carefully removed. The effect is astonishing, almost like a park in its openness. Here is the territory of the Mangbetus. They include sculptors, musicians, boat builders, sorcerers, and wise men. Their way of life is wholly different from that of any other African tribe.

A Mangbetu village is made up of dozens of big round houses with high peaks of thatch, scattered among groups of magnificent shade trees. The white stucco walls are beautifully decorated with designs done in black and brown. Everything is neat and orderly. The red earth has been swept until it is as clean as the floor of a Dutch kitchen.

Wide, well-kept paths wander through bamboo groves. Here and there you see trim buildings with thatched roofs supported by handsomely carved pillars. These are storehouses, workshops, and kitchens where food is prepared for many families at the same time. Here the workers carry on their tasks. Some are making cloth out of bark, staining it with jungle dyes. Others are grinding manioc into flour. This in turn will be cooked into balls like little dumplings.

Tall, bronze figures emerge from the doorways of the houses. The men are dressed in loincloths of pounded bark, striped in black and white and brown. This dramatic costume flares widely at the hips and is drawn tight at the waist by a belt of okapi hide.

The Mangbetu women follow their men, moving in

A Mangbetu has an oval, pointed skull.

stately fashion across the square. Their heads are crowned by halos of braided hair that sway as they walk. Their eyes slant upward at the temples. Ornaments of shining copper wire circle their arms and legs.

Every Mangbetu has a skull that is a high, pointed oval. This is no accident. From the time a baby is only a few months old, his mother is working to shape his head. She binds fibers tightly around his head. These are tightened as the child grows older. At adolescence the head takes on its final shape. Some people claim that this shaping of the skull improves the brain, since the Mangbetus are among the most intelligent of all Congo people. In any case, the process cannot be painful, for the cry of a baby is almost never heard.

One of the outstanding traits of the Mangbetus is the kindness they show toward their children. A visitor never sees a child punished and seldom hears one spoken to crossly. The children have almost perfect manners. They seem friendly and full of fun, happy to be alive.

More than any other, this splendid tribe seems to have conquered the jungle—to have tamed it to a point where a man may live and thrive, in dignity and without fear.

SURVIVAL **IN THE**

JUNGLE

12

TRAVELING IN THE JUNGLE

The jungle areas of the world are vast, and many parts of them are remote from civilization. In order to survive, a person must understand certain basic facts about jungle country.

When you are traveling in a jungle, you must learn how to find water and food in strange country; how to make fire where all wood seems to be wet; how to construct a rainproof shelter out of materials at hand. You must learn how to find your way through trackless country. Above all, you must understand how to take care of your body and conserve its energy. Well-considered preparation is of great importance when an emergency arises. Once you are armed with knowledge of what to expect, no part of the jungle will seem completely hostile or frightening to you.

Survival in the jungle depends on resourcefulness. If you are well equipped and know a few fundamental principles of woodcraft, your chances of survival are excellent. But jungle country is not friendly to man. It is necessary to familiarize yourself also with those things that are harmful and dangerous.

No one should go into the jungle, or fly above it, without at least a minimum of proper equipment. Essentials include lightweight clothing, a good sheath knife or machete, compass, rifle and ammunition, fishhooks and line, matches in waterproof container, and a lightweight poncho. A mosquito head-net is a "must." Such a net folds up no larger than a pocket handkerchief.

Since it is possible to become hopelessly lost within five minutes after leaving a known landmark, a compass always should be carried. In open country during the day it is possible to take bearings from the sun. At night the stars are sure guides to direction. But in most places the jungle rooftop is so dense that it is often impossible to see sun or stars. Even if you are lucky enough to have a map of the region where you are stranded, you must constantly check your position by means of the compass. You must know how to tell where you are at all times.

Keep alert. Watch the ground in front of you carefully. Stop and listen now and again. Avoid haste, rest frequently. In a region of great heat and humidity, the person who sets a fast pace will be the first to succumb to fatigue. A steady, even pace is wisest in the long run.

If you lose your course or trail, don't panic. Try to decide how long it has been since you were sure of your position. Mark the spot where you are with blazes on four sides of a tree—marks that can be seen from any direction. Then you can begin backtracking with the confidence that you can always find the spot from which you started. Except in an emergency, never attempt to travel through the jungle at night.

Whenever possible, it is wise to follow streams and rivers if they are going in your general direction. Native villages are often near the river banks, and animal trails invariably lead to them. Even though the stream may cause you many extra miles of travel, in the end it will save time and energy. Nothing is more exhausting than hacking a trail cross-country through unbroken jungle.

Survival in the Jungle

If a river is broad and deep, without rapids, rafting is an ideal means of travel. Bamboo grows plentifully along the banks of many jungle streams. Since it is hollow and extremely strong, this "grass" tree makes a perfect raft. The bamboo need not be dry: green bamboo floats readily, too.

If possible, avoid high ridges when traveling through jungle country. They are apt to be covered with thickets of thorny rattans—a kind of climbing palm armed with sharp, curved barbs that rip and tear at your clothing. Even with a sharp machete, it is almost impossible to hack a path through a rattan thicket without becoming hopelessly entangled.

Mosquitoes, ticks, and leeches will be your constant companions. The only defense against them is to wear the proper kind of clothing. Shorts should never be worn in the jungle. Trousers must be lightweight and long, the ends tucked into boot tops. If a leech fastens itself to any exposed part of your body, hold a lighted match close to it; the pest will loosen its grip and drop off.

13

FOOD
AND
WATER

Good drinking water is the first necessity to survival in the jungle. Without it, the presence or absence of food is of little importance. Even in tropical rain forest, finding water that is safe to drink can be a problem. Many streams and rivers carry germs that can be deadly to man. Streams found near native villages, even if clear and fresh-looking, are always dangerous. Such water always must be boiled before drinking.

Fortunately, in the jungle there are numerous kinds of water-giving plants and vines that provide a liquid pure and safe. The big rough-barked lianas are one of the best sources of water. Here is the proper way to tap such a vine: reach as high up as you can and cut it off with your knife. Then make a second cut about a foot from the ground. This will give you a water tube several feet long. Remember, it is important to make the first cut at the top. If the cut is made first at the bottom, the water will ascend the vine and most of it will be lost. The section of rough-barked liana should yield more than a pint of clear water. It will be many degrees cooler than the temperature of the air.

Throughout the jungle there are plants known as bromeliads. These are air plants which attach themselves to jungle trees. Their leaves curve upward, forming natural cups that catch and hold rain water. Bromeliads grow in dry jungle areas as well as in wet ones. In the dry regions, where rainfall is scarce, they catch the dew, secreting it in the base of the leaves where it cannot evaporate.

The traveler's palm is another unfailing source of water. This curious tree spreads its broad leaves in the shape of an open fan. At the base of each leaf a man may quench his thirst with a draught of purest water. It is a good thing to remember that water from almost all plants is pure to drink. It will save your time and safeguard your health to make use of such sources. But

The traveler's palm supplies safe drinking water.

vines having a bitter or milky sap should be avoided.

Many jungle plants also furnish food which is much easier to find than animal food. Before going into the jungle, become familiar with as many edible varieties as possible. If you haven't had a chance to do this, watch and see what kind of fruits and nuts the birds and monkeys choose. Such food almost always is safe for a man to eat.

Palm trees of many varieties are found throughout the tropics. They are easily recognized, and many of them

Coconuts can keep a person alive and well.

are sources of nourishment. The most familiar of all is the tall and graceful coconut palm. Robert Louis Stevenson called it the "giraffe of vegetables." Natives of jungle regions prefer the green coconuts to the ripe brown ones which our markets sell at home. The so-called "milk" of the green nut is not milky at all. It is clear and sparkling, thirst-quenching on the hottest day. And the meat of the green nut is soft as gelatin, easily scooped out, and very nutritious.

Coconut trees bear throughout the year. Each tree usually has nuts in all stages of growth. It furnishes the most ready and abundant food. A good tree yields one hundred to three hundred nuts a year, and the mature nuts will keep for months. A person may remain alive and well for a long time on coconuts alone.

Nuts that have fallen to the ground and begun to sprout should be split in half. The base of the sprout is sometimes called "millionaire's salad." Actually the sprout itself is a miniature coconut tree. The marsh-mallow-like substance that fills the space once occupied by the fluid of the nut has a delicate flavor. Baked in the shell, it tastes much like buttered squash.

Slice a coconut in half and lay it in the sun to dry. The result is known as copra. This makes an excellent reserve of concentrated food that will keep for a long time. Or oil may be squeezed out of it—oil to relieve painful sunburn, or to prevent knives and guns from rusting. Copra serves still another purpose in jungle living: pieces of it impaled on a stick make perfect candles. The oily substance burns with a clear yellow flame.

Rattan palms also are a handy source of food. Their growing tips are edible. Moreover, sections of the stem can be cut in short lengths and placed to roast on a bed of coals. When the tough outer covering is well charred, the inner heart will be tender and ready to eat.

Ferns of many descriptions abound in the jungle— low-growing ones that hug the earth and others that grow as trees, thirty or forty feet tall. Most of us never think of ferns as food, but the natives of jungle regions have eaten them for centuries. When boiled, ferns taste much like cucumbers.

Breadfruit is another tree common to tropical regions. The fruit looks like a big green cannonball. The tree's glossy leaves are as large as dinner plates and often are used as such. Boiled or baked, breadfruit tastes like a combination of bread and potatoes. It is highly starchy and filling.

Banana trees are in fruit throughout the year. A single

tree bears only one bunch of bananas. If you cut down the tree to get at the fruit, a new tree will spring up quickly from the roots of the old one. Full-sized green bananas are edible when cooked. Some varieties are unpalatable raw, even when mature. These are cooking bananas, or plantains. They may be distinguished from the true banana by the fruit-bearing stalk, which stands upright.

If you are lucky enough to stumble on a cut-over area of jungle, or an abandoned native garden, you may

Breadfruit, when cooked, tastes like bread and potatoes.

find many different kinds of fruits—guavas, limes, custard apples, and mangoes. And almost certainly there will be wild sweet potatoes or yams.

The yam vine has a heart-shaped leaf. The tuber is a heavy root with a rough brown skin and fine white flesh, which must be cooked. If it is to be baked, cut it into small pieces first. The roots may be eaten raw.

When it comes to seeking animal foods in the jungle, rivers and streams are the likeliest places to hunt. It is not necessary to be familiar with the many different species of birds and mammals, since all are edible. Methods of hunting are similar to those of hunting at home. Try to make your way without being heard, seen, or scented. Hunt either in the early morning or late evening, when wild life is most active.

A sharp watch must be kept for tracks, trails, and feeding marks. But in the jungle you must keep alert also for the pitfalls, the traps and snares which native hunters conceal so cunningly along game trails.

All plants and animals are closely associated in the jungle. A definite order underlies their distribution. Those animals which do not feed on plants prey upon one another. Consequently the very fact that a certain animal is present suggests that its source of food is also somewhere close at hand. That source may mean for you the difference between going to sleep well fed or hungry.

A stream frequented by water snakes is certain to be well stocked with fish, frogs, tadpoles, and crayfish—all sources of energy food. Snakes themselves have nourished many a starving man. A swarm of bees may lead you to the tree where honey is concealed, or to the bee grubs which native dwellers of all jungle countries consider a delicacy. Flying squirrels, macaws, and toucans will show you the way to their supplies of fruit, nuts, seeds, and edible buds.

Monkeys are a fairly easy target for the hunter. Their meat is excellent, scarcely to be distinguished from veal. These animals may be broiled or baked, but the hair should be singed off before cooking. Wild pigs are common and often can be shot at their feeding places. Nor should a hungry man forget that lizards and iguanas make good eating. The reptiles must, of course, first be skinned. The long slender tail muscle is the tastiest bit when roasted on the coals. The easiest way to catch an iguana is by pouring boiling water into its hole in a tree trunk, or setting a noose trap about the opening of the ground holes.

A wild pig can provide meat.

The flying fox (actually a large bat) sleeps by day, hanging from the branches of fruit trees. Thus it is not difficult to capture. The flesh is delicate, tender, and white; but it has a disagreeable odor which can be overcome by wrapping the meat in certain leaves, such as papaya.

At some seasons of the year, turtles come ashore in large numbers to lay their eggs. The eggs are rich and yolky, and parts of the turtle make good eating. Turn a turtle on its back to prevent escape. Cut the throat.

The blood, which can be caught in a coconut shell, is nourishing food after it has been heated and allowed to coagulate.

Small crocodiles are edible, though few men except native forest dwellers relish the coarse meat of these repulsive creatures. Crocodiles should be shot in shallow water, because they sink like stones to the bottom when wounded or killed.

An experienced jungle traveler will be certain to have an assortment of fishhooks and line in his pocket. Fishing methods that work at home are likely to be a success in the jungle. Wood grubs and insects that can be found in any hollow stump may be mashed up and used as bait. Natives make fishhooks from the big thorns of the rattan palms. At certain seasons, many fish abounding in the coastal waters of tropical countries are poisonous. This is caused by some particular poisonous substance on which they feed. But all fish caught in jungle rivers may be safely eaten when thoroughly cooked beforehand.

If food is really scarce, and starvation stares a man in the face, beetle grubs and termite larvae can always be resorted to. Remember, Indians have been eating just such food for centuries!

14

FIRE
AND
SHELTER

For protection against sun, rain, or wind, shelters may be quickly constructed from a number of materials. In regions where coconut trees do not grow, broad ginger leaves or banana leaves, supported on a rough framework, form a protective shelter. Passing banana leaves over heat toughens the leaf and renders it more waterproof.

Before choosing a camp site, consider its convenience for sleeping, for food, and for water. Make a bed up off the ground if possible. Above all, do not sleep in wet clothing on damp ground unless you have no choice in the matter. If a natural shelter exists, such as a cave, use it by all means. The true key to survival in the jungle is to conserve your energy as much as possible.

Many jungle areas become cold at night. It may become necessary to keep a fire going until dawn. In making a fire in the Rain Forest, look for dry kindling under overhanging rocks, or on the under side of leaning trees. If none is available, cut away the wet exterior of dead limbs to get at dry wood. If your matches have

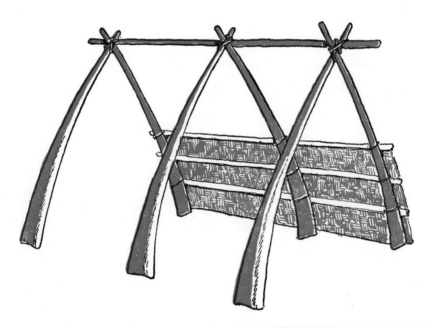

A framework can support a shelter of broad leaves.

become wet, they can be dried by rubbing them rapidly between the palms of your hands.

Sometimes it is necessary to make fire without matches. This can be done by focusing sunlight on a pile of dry tinder through the lens of a flashlight or binoculars. Or sparks struck from a piece of flint or quartz can be used to start a fire. The back of a knife blade, or any piece of hard steel, may be employed to strike the sparks. The paper-like skin that lines the inner wall of bamboo will ignite readily when most other tinders fail.

Wherever the coconut tree abounds, you can save matches by using dry coconut husks. With a lens, the husk can be ignited almost immediately when the sun is overhead. The native method is to split an old, dry coconut in half, and put one end of it into the campfire to set it alight. Natives often carry it with them to the next camp. If they plan to return to the same camp site, they bury a smoldering log in the sand.

Natives do most of their cooking without metal utensils. A jungle survivor can do the same if necessary. An open fire is used for broiling. A ground oven takes care of all other cooking. Though this method is slow, it has the advantage of requiring little attention, and protects the food from flies and other pests. Also it uses relatively little firewood.

To make such an oven, dig a round pit two feet in diameter, and eight to ten inches deep. Drive a stake two feet long into the exact center of the pit. Put a layer of dry leaves and kindling over a layer of springy twigs at the bottom. Cover this with coconut husks and larger sticks. Then lay a dozen or more stones twice the size of your fist on top of the fuel. Remove the stake. Now drop some burning tinder into the bottom of the oven through the opening left by the stake. A slender bamboo tube makes a good bellows to fan the flame. Allow the fire to burn undisturbed for about an hour. The stones will be thoroughly heated by that time.

Next, wrap your meat or fish carefully in leaves. Banana leaves are perfect for this purpose. Lay the food on the smoking stones. Cover it with a thick layer of green leaves to seal in the heat. Within two hours your dinner will be cooked to perfection.

To preserve animal food, recook it once each day. Fish and fruit can be smoked and dried for future use. Boil water by putting it in a bamboo tube or a coconut shell placed above the coals, or by dropping hot stones into the water, one at a time. A doubled-over coconut leaf makes a surprisingly good pair of tongs for this job. Joints of bamboo, sealed at the ends, are also fine containers for cooking meat.

Once you have set up your first shelter and cooked your first meal, your chances of "living off" the jungle for a long time are excellent.

Survival in the jungle is a science. Throughout the jungle world—Brazil, Indonesia, West Africa—the forest peoples have developed this science to perfection. You can learn to do so, too. But you must remain constantly alert. One moment of carelessness could be your undoing. Everything you see and hear and encounter must be interpreted in terms of water, food, fire, and shelter —the basic necessities without which no one can live.

In years to come, the jungles of the world face an uncertain fate. Vast tracts of equatorial forest are being plundered to make way for plantations. Timber is being cut with no thought of planting new trees. Rains erode the treeless earth; the topsoil blows away. Widespread commercial projects, the mining and undermining of the earth, threaten the Rain Forests. Years ago the virgin forests of North America fell before the axes of the pioneers and the demands of the great saw-mills. Now the Rain Forests may disappear within a few generations.

The loss of these rich natural resources will be tremendous. Only wise and far-sighted control can save for future generations this wealth of the jungle and its by-products.

Index

Acacia tree, 92
Adder, 103-04
Aëdes mosquito, 38
Africa, Equatorial, 4, 81-113
African jungle: apes in, 99-101; birds in, 84-85; elephants in, 94-95; Manghetus of, 110-13; Pygmies of, 81, 105-10; snakes in, 103-04; tsetse fly in, 93. *See also* Congo; Ituri Rain Forest
Amazon River, 4, 15, 25, 50, 83
Anaconda, 34
Anopheles mosquito, 38
Anteater: giant, 27-28; silky, 28
Antelope, Malayan, 63
Antivenin, 21
Ants, 10; leaf-cutting, 38; soldier, 30, 38-39; Tucandeiro, 27
Anvil bird, 37
Aspirin, 19

Babassu palm, 18
Bali, 59, 63, 76
Balsa, 18
Bamboo, 10, 59-61, 120
Banana, 126-27
Baobab, 92
Basilisk, 36
Bat, 36-37
Bee, "sweat," 40
Belgian Congo. *See* Congo
Bell bird, 37
Belladonna, 19
Benteng, 66-67
Betel nut, 77
Birdlime, 65-66
Birds: in African jungle, 84; in Brazilian jungle, 26, 36-37; in Indonesian jungle, 63, 74
Boa, land, 34-35
Boar, jungle, 66
Borneo, 53-54, 60, 63, 67-68
Brazil nut, 18
Brazilian jungle, 15-50; birds in, 26, 36-37; extent of, 3-4; government pro-

gram for, 48-49; insects in, 27, 37-40; medicinal plants in, 19-21; monkeys in, 26, 30-31; rubber trees in, 22-25; snakes in, 34-35; temperature of, 5-6; trees in, number of species of, 10, 16; wild life in, 26-40
Breadfruit, 126-27
Bromeliad, 122
Buffalo: African, 99; water, 74
Buprestis beetles, 75
Buriti palm, 18
Burma, 68, 73, 76
Bushmaster, 35
Buta, 91

Calabash, 16
Camphor tree, 59
Canoe, dugout, 42
Capybara, 27
Carabao, 74
Carapato, 40
Cashew tree, 18
Castor bean, 19
Catfish, 33
Cayman, 33
Cebus, 30-31
Cedar, 18
Celebes, 53
Centipede, 10
Central America, jungle in, 4
Chavantes, 25, 50
Chimpanzee, 70, 101
Cinchona tree, 19
Cobra, king, 63
Coca plant, 19
Cocaine, 19
Cocoa, 19
Coconut palm, 124-25, 134
Coffee, 19
Congo, 4, 81-82, 84; elephants in, 94; gorillas in, 99; ivory furnished by, 88-89; wealth of, 88
Congo River, 83, 86; steamer on, 83-84, 86

Index

Index

ABOUT THE AUTHOR-ILLUSTRATOR OF THIS BOOK

Armstrong Sperry's interest in remote parts of the world has taken him on many far-ranging trips. For two years, he traveled the length and breadth of the Pacific Ocean, living among natives of many tribes. He served as assistant ethnologist on a scientific expedition to the South Seas, traveling in a four-masted schooner along the same route taken by Captain James Cook in 1769.

Mr. Sperry has also written and illustrated *All About the Arctic and Antarctic*, as well as three Landmark Books —*Captain Cook Explores the South Seas*, *John Paul Jones*, and *The Voyages of Christopher Columbus*. His book *Call It Courage* received the Newbery Award.